A teacher's handbook
Stonehenge

Carol Anderson, Philippe Planel and Peter Stone

Stonehenge at dawn.

English Heritage

Contents

Introduction

Stonehenge and the cultural environment in which it stands are unique. Nestled within an area of less than two square kilometres are literally hundreds of prehistoric monuments built somewhere between 5000 and 3000 years ago. Within this landscape stand the remains of the stone circle itself, with its huge uprights and lintels of local sandstone and the smaller 'bluestones' – almost certainly transported especially to the site from South Wales, some 385 kilometres (240 miles) away.

The stones and other monuments of this landscape bear silent testimony to a period of the past of which we know very little: a period long before writing had been invented, a period far out of reach of historians. What is known about Stonehenge, its landscape and the people who lived, worked and worshipped here has been painstakingly pieced together by archaeologists who, over the past hundred or so years, have not only studied the remains of the upstanding monuments, but also excavated parts of, and scientifically investigated much of, the surrounding landscape. Thousands of human-made objects and natural environmental remains – including, for example, microscopic pollen, seed and insect remains – have been studied and analysed.

It is through such specialised work that we can begin to tell the story of Stonehenge. We know, for example, that the people who lived here some 3000 to 5000 years ago worked with sophisticated stone, and then metal, tools; that they used pottery containers; that they traded – amongst other things – both these tools and containers over long distances; and that they relied on domesticated plants and animals for a significant amount of their food. We can infer quite securely, that they had begun to live most of the year in one place; that they lived in an extremely complex society; and that they possessed some form of spiritual belief. However, we will never be quite sure of what their homes and other buildings really looked like – or what these were really like inside; nor be sure how often they moved house; or how many fields, sheep or cattle one family would expect to possess – if possession is even a concept they would have understood. We will never know of the rules or traditions that governed their society; nor know their names or the names of their god or gods; or understand the fundamentals of their spiritual or religious beliefs. We can hope, as their material remains continue to

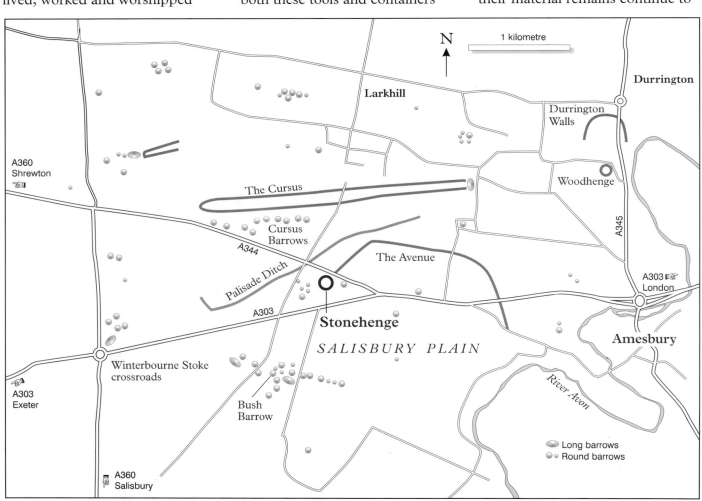

Stonehenge and its environs.

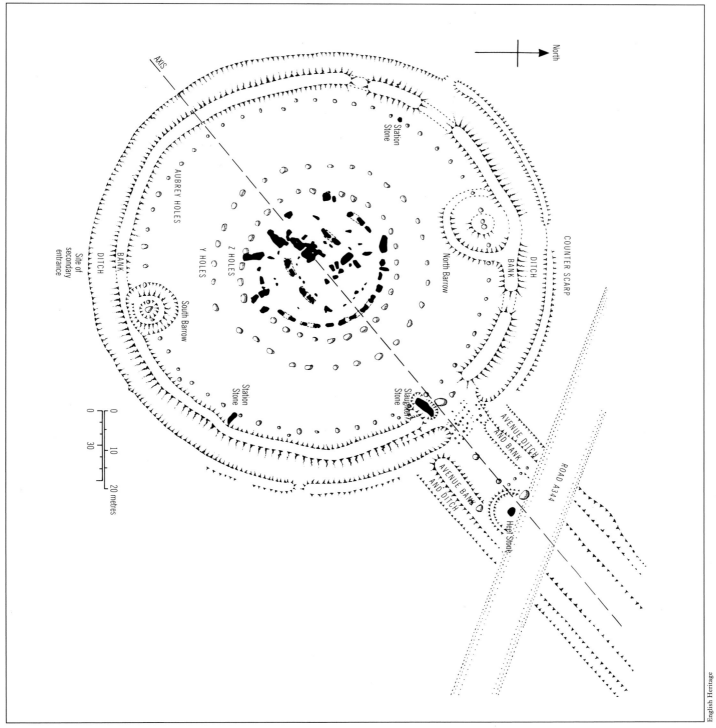

A plan of the Centre Circle and immediate environs.

be studied, that increasingly plausible answers to these and hundreds of other questions will be found.

Recently Stonehenge, designated by UNESCO as a World Heritage Site, has been at the centre of a great debate about how such 'heritage' sites should be managed, interpreted and presented. Part of this debate has focused on who controls the interpretation and presentation of – and access to – the monument.

This handbook therefore not only looks at the prehistoric past of Stonehenge and its builders but also at this intense heritage debate in the belief that children have as much to gain from studying the site in the present as they have in studying it in the past. Stonehenge is England's best known heritage problem or challenge, but the issues which surround it affect many other sites: roads, access, visitor pressure, visitor centres,

planning, the conflicting demands of various groups and more fundamental questions such as who the site *belongs to* and what value(s) we attach to the past – and why. Possibly as a result of discussions provoked by such study, future citizens will be better equipped to participate in decisions that have to be taken about the heritage; and perhaps avoid some of the mistakes present and recent generations have made.

Understanding the site

Stonehenge: a local achievement

The stone circle itself is only one of hundreds of prehistoric monuments that cover this part of Salisbury Plain. We tend to regard it now as the centre of this concentration of monuments but there is no definite proof that this was actually the case for any or part of its history. Archaeologists have discovered the remains of a number of other monuments that may at various times have been equally as, if not more important than, Stonehenge.

The sophisticated construction techniques used at Stonehenge are based on wood technology and use, for example, tongue and groove and mortice and tenon jointing. Given that the builders of Stonehenge could build like this in stone, using only crude stone pounders, we can only guess at what buildings and structures these people made out of wood. Perhaps the builders of Stonehenge were copying quite common structures that already existed in wood. We may never know the answer to this or hundreds of other similar questions.

Until the 1950s archaeologists could not believe that the early inhabitants of Wessex were capable of such building feats, and credited a Mediterranean cultural influence, even Mediterranean craftsmen, with the work. However, in recent decades this view has changed. The scientific dating of organic evidence associated with Stonehenge and other similar monuments has in some cases produced dates earlier than the Mediterranean sites that supposedly influenced their construction. These results coincided with a move away from the theory of diffusion of people and/or ideas from one source (in this case the Mediterranean) as the sole means for innovation and change; a theory replaced with the notion of independent development. In other words, the

This carving on one of the stones may be of a Mycenaean dagger and was used as evidence for Mediterranean influence.

inhabitants of Wessex are now seen as having been quite capable of building Stonehenge without any outside assistance – a view supported by an ever increasing amount of scientific archaeological evidence.

Description of Stonehenge

Stonehenge itself was not built once, used and then abandoned. The monument was designed, built, redesigned and rebuilt over a period of about two thousand years and what we see now are the fragmentary remains of the last of these successive building phases and alterations. The alterations almost certainly reflected changes in, at least, the rituals relating to the spiritual beliefs of the people of

the area and may well have reflected developments or actual changes in the beliefs themselves – changes that almost certainly we shall never fully understand.

We also do not know why Stonehenge was built where it was. It may be that the location was already an important place – at least in traditional memory – as there is some evidence of much earlier activity in the area that predates what is referred to below as Stonehenge I by some thousand years or more. The monument's location may also have been influenced by the ground cover of the period and what could, and could not, be seen from Stonehenge – and, of course, vice versa.

Stonehenge I (c.3050-2900 BC)

The first monument at Stonehenge consisted of a roughly circular ditch (dug in segments with sections of undug chalk remaining as 'causeways' between the segments) about two metres deep. The chalk dug from the ditch was piled up on its inside to form a continuous bank. There was no stone circle. The main entrance to the circle seems to have been at its north east and aligned roughly along the axis of the mid-summer sunrise/mid-winter sunset. A series of 56 round pits, about a metre deep and a metre wide, were dug

Stonehenge I comprised a ditch and bank enclosing the Aubrey holes. There was a main entrance in the north-east roughly on the present alignment and a southern entrance.

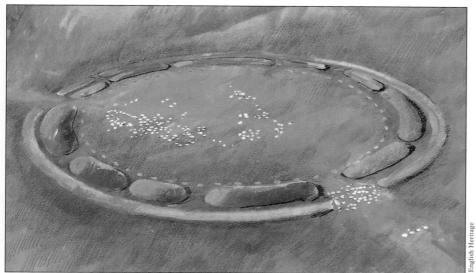

Stonehenge II contained timber settings within the earthwork although it is impossible to know what buildings or structures these formed. In this illustration only the known post-holes have been shown.

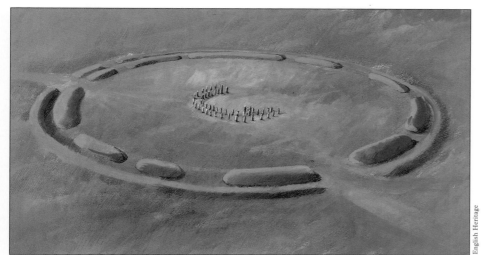

Probably the earliest setting of Stonehenge III with the bluestones arranged in a central crescent.

on the inside of the bank. These pits are known as the Aubrey holes after their seventeenth century discoverer, the antiquarian John Aubrey. Their original purpose is unclear but they may have held wooden posts. Whatever their function, they seem to have been filled in again soon after being dug. The Aubrey holes are now marked by concrete discs set into the grass.

Stonehenge II (c.2900-2600 BC)

The original bank and ditch were cleared of the chalkland scrub that had grown up over what seems to have been a short period of abandonment. A number of post holes (ie holes that have been interpreted as once holding wooden uprights) have been identified around the north eastern entrance. These presumably formed some sort of entrance way into the monument. Archaeologists have found a number of other post holes inside the bank and ditch. Unfortunately, it is impossible to be sure whether all of these were in use at the same time or whether they were part of a structure – or simply individual uprights. A number of the Aubrey holes were partially re-opened and cremated bodies inserted into the chalk fill of the original holes.

A structure of unknown date but

Stonehenge III reached its zenith with the spectacular construction of the huge sarsen circle and the processional Avenue. The principal entrance was marked by the Heel Stone and three Portal Stones. Within the sarsen circle the bluestones were reset in an unknown arrangement. Was the circle ever complete? (see page 10).

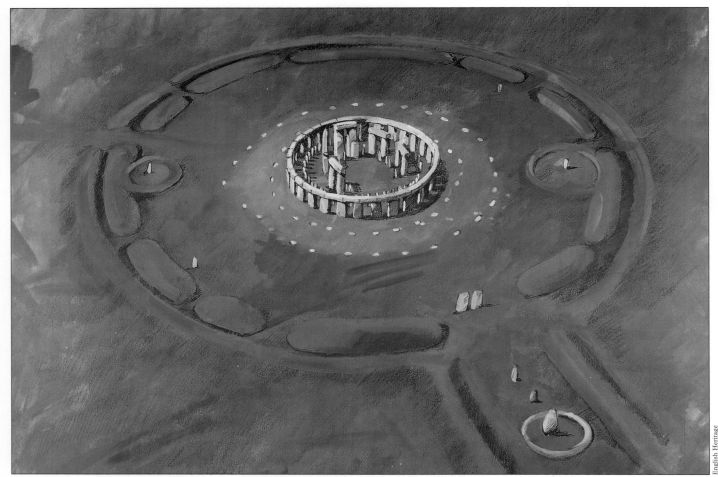

which seems most likely to be associated with this period is known as 'The Palisade Ditch'. This ran to the north of the monument in an east/west direction. Its function is unclear but it may have been some form of territorial marker: either restricting access to, or sight of, Stonehenge from the west – or vice versa.

Stonehenge III (c.2600-1600 BC)

The final phase of Stonehenge comprises the construction of a succession of arrangements of standing stones. It seems that a pair of stones was erected some way outside the north east entrance. Shortly afterwards, one of the stones forming this external entrance was removed. The remaining stone was then provided with its own bank and ditch. This stone is now known as the Heel Stone – probably after a story in which the Devil threw the stone at a friar hitting him on the heel. A pair of large sarsen stones (see below) was also erected at about this time within the north eastern

entrance way to Stonehenge. Only one of these remains. Its partner was probably removed for building stone within the last few hundred years. It is known, for no good reason other than eighteenth-century romanticism, as the 'Slaughter stone'.

Running out from the entrance an avenue consisting of parallel earthen banks about 20 metres apart with ditches on the outside was built. This avenue, which ran on either side of the heel stone, followed the slope away from Stonehenge for about 500 metres before turning east to run down to the River Avon near present day Amesbury. It almost certainly provided an impressive, and somewhat exclusive, ceremonial approach to the site. Most of the avenue that runs down to the River Avon has long since been ploughed away by farming and can only be traced in aerial photographs.

At some stage almost certainly during this period four stones, two enclosed within their own small bank and ditch, were raised just inside the Stonehenge bank. These

The final form of Stonehenge III consisted of the sarsen circle and horseshoe of trilithons, respectively enclosing a circle and horseshoe of bluestones. The Z and Y holes had been dug, but left unfilled.

are now known as the Station stones.

Excavations within the central area have provided a complex and somewhat confused pattern of holes suggesting that there may have been several different arrangements of stones prior to those we can identify with any certainty. What is clear is that about 80 stones weighing about four tonnes each were set up in two horseshoe shapes in the centre of the site. Geologists tell us that these stones, known because of their colouring as the 'bluestones', only occur in one relatively small part of South West Wales in the Preseli Mountains. It is probable that the bluestones were ordered specifically for Stonehenge and transported to the site by land and sea. If this is the case, their ordering and transportation gives an indication of the sophistication and complexity of the society that built the monument. Conversely, some experts have suggested that the bluestones may have been moved to the Stonehenge area much earlier by glacial action but, on balance, especially as there are no other recorded natural occurrences of bluestones within the Stonehenge area, this seems unlikely.

A bluestone appears to have been used in the construction of Boles Barrow (near Heytesbury and about 35 km from Stonehenge). Boles Barrow is a Neolithic burial mound (see below) and dates from before the bluestone period at Stonehenge. The association of a bluestone with this burial mound (the stone was recorded as part of the mound in the nineteenth century but subsequently moved to a new location) suggests an existing tradition of introducing bluestones into the area.

As some of the bluestones have been shaped it is possible that they had been actually fixed together in an earlier, different, arrangement at Stonehenge – or even at a different site. However, if the bluestones were intended to form complete circles this phase of Stonehenge seems never to have been completed.

For whatever reason, the decision seems to have been taken not to finish this bluestone monument. Instead, a completely different monument, using much larger stones brought from the Marlborough Downs some 30kms (20 miles) away, was constructed. These 'sarsen' stones are much larger than the bluestones and weigh between 30 and 50 tonnes each. The name 'sarsen' dates from at least the seventeenth century and is probably derived from the medieval word Saracen – implying connotations of foreignness and paganism. Similar stones had been used over 500 years before to construct the much larger but less technologically sophisticated ceremonial site at Avebury (see Bibliography and resources). The Stonehenge stone circle is unique. Its stones were set up in a circle with each pair apparently capped by a lintel stone also of sarsen. Inside this circle stood five pairs of enormous sarsen stones or trilithons (the

English Heritage

largest remaining example weighing 45 tonnes and standing 6.7 metres [22 ft] high) which were also capped by their own lintels. All of the sarsen stones have been shaped by being pounded by workers using small round hammer stones – many of which have been found during excavations in the area and which were also used as packing stones when the huge sarsens were finally erected. The upright sarsens were intentionally tapered – presumably to create the optical illusion that the stones are higher than they are. The lintels of the outer circle all had to be slightly

The tallest sarsen, the remaining upright of the central trilithon, weighs over 45 tonnes and is 22 feet high. It may have weighed twice this before it was shaped on site. Its fallen lintel lies in front. The mortice and tenon jointing can be seen clearly.

curved to fit together to form the circle. In addition they were shaped at their ends to fit together with tongue-and-groove joints and on their underside small round depressions were cut to accept corresponding protrusions on the tops of the sarsen uprights – mortice-and-tenon jointing.

At the same time about 20 of the bluestones from the dismantled

A possible method of erecting one of the sarsen trilithons.

earlier monument were reused in an oval setting within the sarsen circle. Two series of pits (known as the Y and Z holes) were dug outside the sarsen circle which may have been intended to house the rest of the dismantled bluestone monument. However, something made those in charge change their minds yet again and the circles of pits seem never to have been completed and the remaining bluestones never erected in them. Instead, the oval arrangement of bluestones was taken down and replaced by a horseshoe arrangement of bluestones at the very centre of the monument (inside the sarsen trilithons) and the remaining bluestones were erected in a circle between the sarsen circle and the sarsen trilithons.

How Stonehenge was built

The transportation of the bluestones from South Wales and the much heavier sarsens from the Marlborough Downs, their shaping and eventual erection is clear evidence of enormous effort and organization. The bluestones were almost certainly moved by water as much as possible but a significant amount of their journey – and all of the corresponding journey of the sarsens – had to be overland. There is no definite evidence of how the stones were moved but it seems probable that they were pulled on wooden sledges. Until recently it had always been assumed that human power was used to pull these sledges but recent authorities suggest that draft animals – already almost certainly employed to cultivate the land – may well have been used.

Once at Stonehenge the stones had to be shaped. This was done by pounding them with small sarsen stones about the size of footballs. All the shaping and most of the initial joinery work would have been done with the stones on the ground before they were erected. The final joinery work on the sarsens was probably carried out in situ as the stones would have had to settle in their holes before the lintels were put in place.

Fallen and dangerously leaning stones have been re-erected in two major conservation programmes this century. From archaeological evidence found during this work, from the experience of the work itself, and from experimental archaeology, where archaeologists have attempted to move and erect stone using prehistoric technology, the most likely methods of stone erection and lintel placement have been suggested. These are explained in the diagrams above.

Experimental archaeology in practice: schoolboys working with Professor Stuart Atkinson pull a stone in the 1950s. Recent authorities believe animal, not human, power was used to move the stones.

English Heritage

A monument constantly changing

Stonehenge was in use as some form of ritual monument for over two thousand years. Unfortunately, we will never be able to infer what it actually looked like for most of that time. For example, we do not – and almost certainly never will – know whether the wooden posts of Stonehenge II formed part of a building; whether they were rough, unworked uprights (effectively small tree trunks) or intricately carved (and painted?) columns or totem poles. As the brief description of Stonehenge III above indicates, during the period of its use there were major changes in the physical appearance of the monument and – seemingly – significant changes of mind as building was actually in progress. Why the Z and Y holes were apparently dug to take the remaining bluestones but never used will remain a mystery for ever. Equally, even those things that appear on first sight to be easily understood have complications. For example, while it appears that the builders of Stonehenge III

(Right) The side of this sarsen stone has been dressed by hammering shallow grooves to remove its rough surface.

(Below) Some of the football sized stones used for hammering.

English Heritage

English Heritage

An air photograph of Stonehenge in 1935. Note the custodian's cottage and Stonehenge café on either side of the A344 on the left of the picture, and the buildings of a pig farm just above Stonehenge. The line of the Avenue can be seen clearly.

One of numerous nineteenth-century engravings of Stonehenge.

intended the outer circle of sarsens to have a continuous lintel capping, on closer inspection it seems that this may never have been the case as, in at least one instance, one of the paired stone uprights is far too short to have ever been capped with its partner. There is no evidence to suggest that the present short stone has replaced an original taller one, nor that it has had anything broken from its height – although if this happened in antiquity there would be little evidence of such damage today. It therefore may be that the outer circle was never completed with a full set of lintels. Does this mean that the builders failed in their task to find enough suitable sarsens and therefore botched their job; or that there was some important ritual significance in an incomplete circle; or that the stone has lost its top half at some time in the past? We shall never know.

Other monuments in the Stonehenge landscape

The Stonehenge landscape was central to the lives of the builders of Stonehenge and it is now central to the future of Stonehenge (see page 3). In years to come it may seem incredible that people in the twentieth century allowed the stone circle to be separated from its associated prehistoric landscape and monuments and cut off from its ceremonial avenue by a busy road for so long. Alternatively, people in the future may wonder why we were so concerned with preserving the incomprehensible remains of lost civilizations at all.

The Avenue, however, is only one of hundreds of other prehistoric monuments in the area. The most common are barrows or burial mounds. These lie everywhere around Stonehenge, and comprise the greatest remaining concentration of such monuments in Britain. The long barrows are the earliest type and, since they are dated to between 4000-3000BC, most of them predate even the earliest stage at Stonehenge.

Far more common are the various types of round barrow, categorised by archaeologists as bowl, bell, disc, and pond. These date from the Bronze Age and may contain the remains of those members of the ruling elite responsible for the building of the bluestone and sarsen phases of Stonehenge. Many of the rich grave goods found in these burials by early archaeologists are displayed in Devizes and Salisbury museums and are well worth seeing as they give a clear insight into the wealth and wide range of skills available to (at least a certain section of) Bronze Age society. Round barrows are usually gathered in distinctive groups or cemeteries. The closest cemetery is known as Cursus Barrows, and lies between Stonehenge and the cursus (see plan of the area on page 2). The cursus itself is a long, linear earthwork of which a number of other examples exist throughout Britain. It consists of two parallel banks and ditches closed and rounded off at its west end by a later round barrow. It is aligned to the east on an earlier or contemporary long barrow. The function of these monuments is not at all clear. As they do not seem to have any clear practical function most archaeologists suggest that they may be some form of ritual monument – but this really is only a best guess at this stage. They have been dated to the middle Neolithic period (see Life at Stonehenge) and thus – if it was a ritual monument – the cursus may have provided an important focus even before Stonehenge I was built.

Within the same landscape, but not within easy walking distance, lie two very important monuments north-east of Stonehenge: Durrington Walls and Woodhenge. Durrington Walls is a huge circular bank and ditch, several hundred metres across, now bisected by the A345. During road improvements in the 1960s archaeologists recovered evidence of two very large and impressive timber buildings within this monument. Little remains to be seen of Durrington Walls other than a low bank on either side of the A345. Woodhenge as its name suggests, is a henge monument made of wooden rather than stone uprights; post holes are what actually survive. Both of these monuments were in use at the time of Stonehenge. The arrangements of post holes found during excavation at Woodhenge are indicated on site by modern concrete posts set up by the excavators in the 1930s. These have themselves now become of some interest in the history of interpretation of field monuments!

(Above)
A view from above the sarsen circle showing the curve of the lintels.

(Below)
A view of the centre circle. The bluestone in the foreground has had a groove cut along its length, possibly to fix it with another stone in an earlier arrangement.

English Heritage

English Heritage

Timeline

A floodlit Stonehenge. The police have requested that the stones not be floodlit at night to avoid the possibility of accidents on the A303.

c 3050-2900 BC
Stonehenge I – bank and ditch and Aubrey holes

c 2900-2600 BC
Stonehenge II – A wooden structure of some kind is erected within the original bank and ditch

2500BC   2000BC   1500BC   1000BC

c AD 200
Roman visitors drop coins

c 2600-1600 BC
Stonehenge III – Construction of stone structures, initially of bluestones from Wales with later additions of sarsen stones from the Marlborough Downs; construction of the Avenue

AD 1130
Henry of Huntingdon's description of the stones (see page 14)

Artist's impression of the construction of the sarsen stage of Stonehenge III.

AD 1919-1926
Excavations and consolidation work carried out by the archaeologist Colonel William Hawley

Colonel Hawley's consolidation work in progress.

AD 1990s
Planning for new visitor facilities and possible closure and re-routing of roads

AD 1985
National Trust refuse permission for Stonehenge festival

AD 1899/1900
Stone falls – the stone apparently fell in the last minute, of the last day, of the last year, of the nineteenth century

AD 1835
Constable's painting of Stonehenge

AD 1797
A stone falls (see page 15)

AD 1719
Stukeley begins his major investigations of Stonehenge (see page 15)

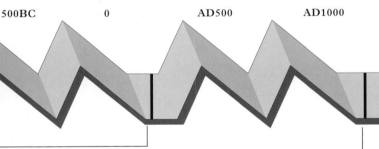

500BC   0   AD500   AD1000   AD1500

AD 1913
Stonehenge protected and scheduled as an ancient monument

AD 1918
Stonehenge offered to the nation by Cecil Chubb owner of the land (the Office of Works became responsible for the stones)

AD 1958
Excavations and consolidation work carried out by Professor Stuart Atkinson

A schoolboy studies an excavation drawing during the 1958 season.

AD 1960
New car park built; followed by underpass and present entrance building (1968)

The entrance in the 1960s.

AD 1984
English Heritage take over responsibility for the monument. Immediately commission a report on the provision of new visitor facilities

Looking at documentary sources

Stonehenge is a prehistoric site and so, by definition, no documentary sources exist from the period the stones were in use. This fact greatly impeded early antiquaries who were only slowly developing fieldwork techniques and were inclined to rely on legend. This means that none of the following sources reflects the past prehistoric reality of Stonehenge, only views about Stonehenge in various historic periods or 'presents'.

"Staneges, where stones of wonderful size have been erected after the manner of doorways, so that doorway appears to have been raised upon doorway; and no one can conceive how such great stones have been so raised aloft, or why they were built there."

1130 Henry of Huntingdon (translated from the Latin). Our first documentary mention of Stonehenge and slightly confusing in that Stonehenge never consisted of two stories.

1136 Geoffrey of Monmouth (translated from the Latin). Thus Stonehenge is woven into Arthurian myth and legend; this account was copied and modified over the years. Clearly no ordinary people could have built this monument, certainly not our 'primitive' ancestors – a view that, until recently, even some archaeologists agreed with. ☞

"Stonehenge was a monument erected in the reign of Aurelius Ambrosius by Merlin to perpetuate the treachery of Hengist, the Saxon general; who having desired a friendly meeting with Vortigern, at the monastery of Amesbury, assassinated him, with four hundred and sixty of his barons and consuls."

"Send for the Giants' Round (says Merlin) which is on Mount Killarus in Ireland. In that place there is a stone construction which no man of this period could ever erect, unless he combined great skill and artistry... If they are placed in position round this site, in the way they are put up over there, they will stand for ever ..."

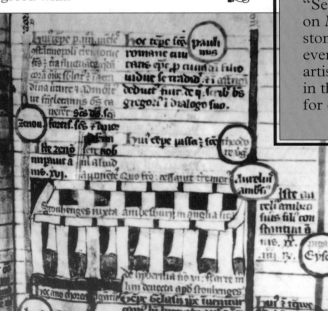

Master and Fellows of Corpus Christi College, Cambridge

One of the earliest illustrations of Stonehenge from a fourteenth-century history of the world.

"although they stande a hondred yeares, hauyng no reparacion nor no solidacion of morter, yet there is no wynde nor wether that doth hurte or peryshe them".

"Almost everything that is related about the bringing of these stones from Ireland is fictional. For everybody, however ignorant, ought to know that these enormous stones – which our own age so short of talent, is unable to shift – were brought by Merlin from some quarry nearby ... It would have been beyond the ability of the Romans to move things of such weight from Ireland to Amesbury."

 1534 Polydore Vergil.

1540 John Leland. Leland completed the first general survey of England. The Irish dimension is roundly attacked, but the mythical Merlin is retained as a historical figure.

"who cast their Eyes upon this Antiquity, and examine the same with Judgement, must be forced to confess it erected by People, grand masters of the Art of Building...whereof the Ancient Britons utterly ignorant..... I conceive Stonehenge to have been erected after the Tuscan order of architecture, and open to heavens and dedicated to the god Coelus."

☞ **1652** Inigo Jones (spelling modernised). James I had commissioned Inigo Jones to investigate Stonehenge following a royal visit to the stones. Jones concluded that Stonehenge was Roman, and even claimed to have identified common design elements between Stonehenge and Roman buildings. To Jones the 'Ancient Britons' were clearly incapable of such a feat – although some critics of Jones suggested (for the first time) a far more remote date for Stonehenge.

"These antiquities are so exceeding old that no bookes doe reach them, so that there is no way to retrieve them but by comparative antiquitie, which I have writt upon the spott, from the Monuments themselves."

☞ **1663** John Aubrey. Aubrey's field work and recording, under royal patronage, was the first serious attempt to break out from what could only be an arid controversy about Stonehenge based on documentary records, concerning a period about which no documentary records survive. Aubrey based his arguments on the standing remains themselves and their distribution. He argued that 'Temples' such as Stonehenge existed in parts of the country where Romans and subsequent invaders had never penetrated, thus they must be works of the British. It is at this point that the Druids first appear in the Stonehenge story. Tacitus had written about the Druids and their rites when describing the Roman conquest of Britain. However, there is absolutely no evidence or reason to link the Druids in any way to Stonehenge. In fact the little that we do know about Druidic religion strongly suggests they did not build substantial monuments – preferring to practice their beliefs in natural sites. The modern Druids' claims to Stonehenge are entirely spurious.

"When you enter the building, whether on foot or horseback and cast your eyes around, upon the yawning ruins, you are struck into an ecstatic reverie, which none can describe, and they only can be sensible of it that feel it. Other buildings fall by piece meal, but here a single stone is a ruin, and lies like the haughty carcase of Goliath. Yet there is as much of it undemolished, as enables us sufficiently to recover its form, when it was in its most perfect state. There is enough of every part to preserve the idea of the whole."

☞ **1740** William Stukeley (spelling modernised). For Stukeley no moment at Stonehenge was a wasted one. He revelled in his work and his interest paid off, no one carried out better fieldwork for the next century. He discovered the cursus, for which no better name has since been found, and the avenue. Stukeley was now by no means the only visitor at Stonehenge and he comments on those who chipped away at the stones for souvenirs. Unfortunately Stukeley's 'reverie' came to dominate him in later life and he began to see Druids everywhere, including in his own person.

1797 *Gentleman's Magazine* (spelling modernised). These stones, one of the trilithons, fell because a hole had been dug behind one of them to provide shelter. This is the first recorded fall of a stone. ☞

"On the third of the month already mentioned [January] some people employed at the plough, full half a mile distant from Stonehenge, suddenly felt a considerable concussion, or jarring of the ground, occasioned, as they afterwards perceived, by the fall of two of the largest stones and their impost."

"The wind played, playing upon the edifice, produced a booming tune, like the note of some gigantic one-stringed harp... The eastward pillars and their architraves stood up blackly against the light, and the great flame-shaped Sun-stone beyond them; and the Stone of Sacrifice midway."

☞ **1889** Thomas Hardy (*Tess of the d'Urbevilles*). Tess enjoys her last moments of freedom at Stonehenge. There are many, many literary and artistic references to Stonehenge (see Chippindale's monumental *Stonehenge Complete*).

A page from a magazine published in the 1920s. The ownership of Stonehenge has been a hotly debated topic for a number of years. ☞

A MAP SHOWING THE GROUND (PLOT C) ADJOINING STONEHENGE, AND INCLUDING THE ANCIENT CURSUS AND AVENUE, NOW MENACED BY THE BUILDER; WITH PLOTS A AND B, ALREADY ACQUIRED FOR THE NATION FOR £8000 EACH.

1930: THE GREAT STONE CIRCLE, WHICH HAS STOOD FOR THE HEART OF SALISBURY PLAIN, SEEN IN ITS SOLITARY GRANDEUR AGAINST THE SUN.

STONEHENGE IN 1930? A DREADFUL VISION OF WHAT MIGH PRESENT APPEAL WERE TO FAIL, AND THE LAND IMMED THE MONUMENT WERE SOLD AS "A DESIRABLE BUIL.

> "Every age has the Stonehenge it deserves."

☞ **1967** Jacquetta Hawkes (archaeologist). This was a prophetic statement in view of the recent conflicts at Stonehenge, when Stonehenge became the sharp edge of a number of social issues: pop festivals, travellers, freedom of movement, policing a democratic society.

> "Wessex without Mycenae."

☞ **1969** Colin Renfrew (archaeologist). This was the title of Renfrew's paper in which he argued that the dagger carving on the stones could not be used as evidence for Mycenean craftsmen at Stonehenge. This finally rid archaeologists of the need to find outside influence for the building of our greatest monument.

> "Stonehenge is not a dry old relic, but a living, moving place raising such passions that it makes human beings rush around in hundreds, causing each other immense trouble and turning sometimes to physical violence. It will leave at least one lasting legacy, in the provisions in the new Public Order Act that will radically change the legal freedom of crowds to gather and move."

> "We come to Stonehenge because in an unstable world it is proper that the people should look for stability to the past in order to learn for the future...Holy land is holy and our right to be upon it cannot be denied."

☞ **1988** Christopher Chippindale (archaeologist).

☞ **1978** Sid Rawle (letter to The Times). Sid Rawle was an unofficial spokesperson for the unofficial free Stonehenge pop festivals.

1990 Peter Fowler (archaeologist). A number of archaeologists have been sympathetic to the claims of people who regard the stones as spiritually rather than touristically or archaeo-logically, important to them. ☞

> "There really has been no understanding that 'nomads' need a resting place... Behind the beards and the long hair, the bedraggled clothes and nudity, the ramshackle vehicles, and the smells, was a simple, social need unknown to the rest of society and quite incomprehensible to those who live a static life... Every acre is owned, and valued; 'travellers' whatever their main or motivation are by definition suspect."

☞ **1994** Colin Renfrew (*Stonehenge – The Great Debate*).

> "Moreover the state of Stonehenge today is a 'national disgrace' – not through the fault of English Heritage which looks after it, nor of the National Trust which holds the great wealth of surrounding sites, but through the failure of government agencies to agree on its future... It has been badly served of late with no visitor centre to provide for the millions of visitors who are bewildered to find the site so badly provided for."

Life at Stonehenge

The Stonehenge landscape in the past

It is difficult today to imagine that the open downland around Stonehenge was once predominately forest. In this state the area provided game, plants, nuts and fruits for hunter-gatherer bands over a period of many thousands of years. There is increasing environmental evidence to suggest that a good deal of woodland clearance took place while people were still largely hunter-gatherers (a process identified archaeologically by declining levels of tree pollen). However, it was only comparatively recently, in what archaeologists call the Neolithic period (between about 4000 and 2200 BC), that human communities begin to radically transform this environment and create – what we could immediately identify today as – a human-made landscape. We should always remember that terms such as Neolithic and Bronze Age are useful chronological markers rather than hard and fast divisions of how people lived. For example, flint continued to be used as a raw material for tools throughout the Bronze Age, while hunting and gathering continued to be an important food resource throughout prehistory and beyond.

The Neolithic

Archaeologists usually identify the Neolithic by the domestication of animals and arable crops. The change from hunting and gathering to farming as the major source of subsistence brought with it the need for people to live in the same place for longer periods as fields, crops and animals needed tending. However, to begin with at least, and certainly until the useful properties of manure were discovered, people probably moved around every few years as the freshly cleared land would have been rapidly exhausted.

Not all woodland was removed: there is still tree pollen in the environmental record and the large quantities of pig bones found during excavation indicate quite extensive areas of woodland (as most pigs were still wild woodland animals). Well managed – possibly coppiced – woodland also provided fuel, tools, raw material for domestic objects, building and fencing material – all essential elements for a settled way of life.

The most common arable crops were wheat and barley. Flax was also grown. The ground would have been prepared either with an ard – an early form of plough without a board to turn the soil – or simple plough. Both of these would almost certainly have been pulled by domesticated oxen. Flint blades hafted into wooden shafts and identified as sickles, have been found on a number of excavations. One of the main uses for the crops was presumably for making bread and pieces of saddle quernstones are common finds.

The majority, about two thirds, of animal bone found on sites of this period is from cattle. Most of the rest of the bones are from pigs and sheep/goat – the bones of the latter two being almost impossible to differentiate. There is some evidence for domesticated dog but none for domesticated cat.

People would have continued to collect wild foods such as hazel nuts and crab apples, the remains of which are frequently found during excavation, and also the full range of indigenous berries, fruits and many plants that still grow today but that are not now used extensively as food, such as nettles and dandelions. Wild animals that seem to have been hunted to supplement the domesticated diet include red deer, horse, pig, cat, fox, wolves and – in the more remote areas of the country – bear. Every part of the animals would have been used as clothes, containers or parts of tools.

People were probably quite aware of how to make pottery vessels when they were hunting and gathering, but it was only in the early Neolithic that pottery containers became very common. Before people settled down such fragile – and relatively heavy – containers would have been too easily and too frequently broken during the constant moving in search of food and game. As the

Artist's impression of the Stonehenge landscape at the time of Stonehenge I.

English Heritage

An early Neolithic pot. This type of pot is known as 'baggy ware' and is thought to imitate the shape of leather containers.

period progressed pottery shapes and styles became increasingly sophisticated, moving from seemingly purely practical containers with no decoration, that may have imitated leather bags in shape, to variously shaped and beautifully decorated vessels.

Limited environmental evidence for arable farming together with a high occurrence of cattle bone has led to the suggestion that the society that constructed Stonehenge I was primarily a pastoralist one, with the cultivation of crops playing a minor role in the population's subsistence. If correct, this would support the idea that there was probably still quite a lot of seasonal movement in search of fresh grazing. Evidence from excavation shows a wide age-range for the domesticated animals. This in turn suggests that there was ample winter grazing and/or fodder, otherwise some of the older animals would probably have been slaughtered.

By the time Stonehenge II was constructed environmental evidence suggests that this relationship was changing and that arable crops were becoming an increasingly important part of the subsistence strategy of the local population.

Recently it has been suggested that sites such as Durrington Walls, just to the north east of Stonehenge, previously thought to contain only ceremonial buildings, may have been settlement sites. While there is some limited evidence of settlement within the area for both early phases of Stonehenge, including the remains of early field systems, good evidence for houses and settlements of the kind used by the builders of these early phases must be drawn from elsewhere. Broadly speaking settlements seem to have been small, scattered, and probably either seasonal or inhabited on a longer term cyclical basis. We can assume people would come together for certain communal gatherings and tasks such as seasonal festivals and markets and, of course, the construction of large ritual monuments. 'Monument' is a modern catch-all term which may not always reflect prehistoric reality. We call long barrows, henges, cursuses and some other visible remains 'monuments' because we do not yet fully

Artist's impression of the Stonehenge landscape about 2000BC. The land has been largely cleared of trees. Chalk burial mounds of local chiefs on be seen on the skyline.

understand their various – and probably varied – function(s).

For example, it is clear that long barrows were associated with death as most, but not all, long barrows contain burials. The majority of burials seem to have been of disarticulated bones (ie bones – and seemingly selected ones at that – not bodies, were buried). However, that is as far as objective interpretation can take us. The bodies of the deceased may have been left out on platforms to decompose before burial – itself only one stage of a complicated funerary rite that may have included bones of ancestors taking part in spiritual ceremonies. It cannot be said definitely whether long barrows were family tombs or whether they were used by some other social grouping. We can scratch at the surface of Neolithic spirituality and funerary rites but we will never fully understand them.

The Bronze Age

The Stonehenge we see today is essentially a Bronze Age monument. The archaeological record shows considerable change in the Bronze Age though this change mainly relates to how richer people were buried rather than how ordinary people lived. A new tradition of burying complete (recently deceased) individuals in round barrows, often grouped in cemeteries, replaced the Neolithic tradition of interring the bones of decomposed individuals in communal long barrows. The individuals whose graves these round barrows mark were almost certainly high status as they were buried with grave goods requiring careful and skilled craftsmanship that reflects the great wealth of the owner. One of the richest of these burials is the Bush Barrow burial from the Wilsford cemetery just south of Stonehenge; it contained three daggers, one with intricate gold work along with other gold objects such as a belt hook, as well as objects of bronze and bone. Although these burials

Beaker pots such as this one used to be thought to indicate large scale human invasion.

demonstrate that Bronze Age society could support specialised craftspeople who would be spared back-breaking agricultural work, grave goods are often just that, goods made for graves rather than for everyday use. Manure for fields rather than gold for graves may actually have been just as important in the lives of most Bronze Age families around Stonehenge. Manure made it possible to cultivate the fields which appeared about the time of Stonehenge III, with permanent boundaries and paths and tracks leading through them and to them – effectively the taming or domestication of the landscape. The period therefore seems to have brought together two essential elements for major communal works: a clearly dominant group in society, as signified by the very rich burials, and an agricultural regime that freed large numbers of people to work on such projects when not needed for agricultural labour.

The Bronze Age is also associated with a new form of pottery, known as Beaker ware. It used to be thought that Beaker pottery indicated the arrival of new people into the area – the 'Beaker folk.' However, the current view is that there was probably large scale movement of artefacts and ideas, without large movements of population, just as, for example, the idea of eating take-away burgers from McDonalds has spread from the United States without a corresponding mass immigration of American citizens.

Intensive field survey around Stonehenge has revealed scatters of

Grave goods of gold, bronze and bone from an early Bronze Age burial mound.

flint dating from this period: such scatters are indicative of activities, for example tool-making, rather than, necessarily, settlement. Flint is known to have been mined in the Stonehenge area. Mined flint is superior to surface flint for the manufacture of tools such as scrapers, knives, arrowheads and axes as it can be worked more easily and effectively.

It is from the Bronze Age that we have strong direct evidence for the first time of at least one place near Stonehenge where people lived. Remains of a farmstead were found during road construction at Winterbourne Stoke crossroads, about two kilometres west of Stonehenge. Here the ground plans of two huts, each visible as a circle of small post holes about seven metres across, were revealed. Their walls were of wattle and daub with a roof covered in thatch. Such farmsteads would also have had outbuildings for both animals and food storage.

A nineteenth-century outing to Stonehenge by bicycle.

Stonehenge since the Bronze Age

Gradually Stonehenge lost its meaning for those for whom the stones still formed part of their daily life. Oral tradition may have preserved something of its former role for a number of generations, but by the time we reach the first recorded historical mention of the monument it was no more than a curiosity (see documentary sources). The area was used for grazing through the Roman and Medieval periods but came under the plough again in the eighteenth century. By this time the stones had not only lost their original meaning but also the respect of the local community, despite various legends attributing supernatural powers to them. Local farmers and road builders used Stonehenge as a quarry. The first tourists also chipped away at the stones to collect souvenirs.

In the nineteenth century the landscape acquired a few plantations and large tracts of land were purchased by the military who built camps and airfields around Stonehenge Down. Some of these have since been removed, others extended. By this time it had become a matter of record when a stone fell down and it was shortly after such an incident that

the then owner of the stones put up a fence around them and imposed a relatively high entrance fee. It seems that the stones only fell over because they had been undermined by 300 years of uncoordinated pit digging and stone removal.

In 1915 Stonehenge was auctioned. It fell to a Cecil Chubb who bought it for his wife who, over breakfast that morning, had said she would like to own it. In 1918 Cecil Chubb gave Stonehenge to the nation. He was subsequently knighted.

In the twentieth century the wheel has come full circle; conservation and even restoration of the monument has, in the latter part of the century, given way to a desire to restore the remains of the monument to its landscape. Perhaps most surprising of all, some people have credited the builders of Stonehenge with detailed astronomical knowledge for which there is no real evidence, while others have claimed Stonehenge as a shrine and have restored spiritual meaning to the stones, something which was unthinkable during the many centuries when Christianity claimed total allegiance in this part of the world.

Educational approaches

Prehistory and learning

One of the most frustrating – and stimulating – things about studying prehistory is that we can rarely be entirely sure we have interpreted the remaining evidence correctly. So much has been lost of the essential elements of everyday life that trying to say what life was like has been compared to doing a thousand piece jigsaw – with no picture as a guide and of which over eight hundred pieces have been lost! For example, we may suggest from the excavation of groups of post holes, interpreted as houses, that houses seem to have been predominantly rectangular in the Neolithic and round in the Bronze Age. However, we have no clear idea if they were constructed of untreated wooden uprights or if such uprights had been intricately carved and perhaps even coloured with natural paints. We have little idea with what – if any – internal wooden furniture such houses would commonly have been fitted out; nor if there were woven wall hangings or other decorations made from materials that do not usually survive. We do not know if people slept on the floor next to their cooking hearths or on raised wooden structures or even in hammocks slung from the rafters. All these things, and many more, can only be inferred at present until, at some time in the future, excavation of a waterlogged site (where wood and other organic materials tend to be much better preserved) may give a deeper insight into such questions.

Nor do we know much about what people wore or what they really looked like. We do know that physically they were just like us – although almost certainly fitter and stronger from their outdoor life. A newly born Neolithic baby would be indistinguishable from a new-born today. Little bits of evidence, including small fragments of woven cloth, that are being pulled together from all over Europe are

Artist's impression of the inside of a Neolithic house.

A model of a Neolithic man split down the middle to indicate two different possible views of what life was like.

beginning to allow archaeologists to infer what people wore. However, there is still little hard and fast evidence of what most normal people looked like as they went about their everyday work, or of what they wore on special occasions, although much has been learnt about clothing from the remains of a Neolithic man found in the Alps in 1991. Whether men and women had distinctively different forms of dressing; whether dress indicated status or group allegiance; how people wore their hair; whether people commonly painted, marked or tattooed themselves: all these and many more are questions that may never be answered.

A recent attempt to put this dilemma over to non-specialists was made at the Alexander Keiller Museum in Avebury. Here a full scale model of a man was created, but instead of being dressed in one set of clothes he was split down the middle and given two different personas. There is nothing on the figure that goes against the archaeological evidence known for the period: there is nothing anachronistic. It is quite possible that both sides of the figure have things that are right about them and perhaps subconsciously the designer may have illustrated the man's everyday work clothes and his 'Sunday best'. The point to make is, that unless archaeologists are lucky enough to find completely unique discoveries such as the man in the ice (see above) that most such inferences about much of prehistory are just that: educated guesses. A point that anyone studying the period must always remember.

For example, some school textbooks state quite categorically that pottery manufacture was carried out by women until specialist male potters took over and began to produce high quality wares. Such changes in production, and their associated social implications, would be very interesting to know about but there is no archaeological evidence to support such assumptions, nor is it easy to see what evidence could be found to indicate the gender of a potter! Such guesswork only serves to paint a stereotypical picture of prehistory that may bear no actual relationship to reality.

It is this lack of clear evidence that, perhaps initially surprisingly, makes prehistory a really valuable tool for teachers. When studying prehistory children are effectively studying the interpretations of archaeologists. Such interpretations are constantly open to re-interpretation and revision as soon as new sites are excavated or new scientific techniques mastered: for example, the radio carbon technique of dating effectively destroyed the theory that Stonehenge was built as the result of influence from the Mediterranean. Once children have accepted the limitations of archaeological evidence, that frequently there is no correct answer, and that what we read about prehistory is someone's *construction* of what they think the past may have been like from such limited evidence, the children too can join in such controlled speculation, for example, get them to discuss what archaeological evidence there could be to indicate the gender of potters, as long as they keep within the confines of what is known archaeologically. Through the painstaking construction of their own interpretations of given events or periods of prehistory, children can quickly come to terms with bias and other problems that dog historical interpretation.

Stonehenge and the whole curriculum

Art

Stonehenge has inspired generations of artists (see Chippindale's *Stonehenge Complete* for a wide selection). Much of the two-dimensional art shows Stonehenge in different seasons or climatic conditions but another interesting aspect is the allegorical use of Stonehenge: the stones crop up in the most unlikely places as a symbol of the unknown or unknowable and in literally hundreds of adverts – interestingly as both symbols of technological

Artist's impression of Stonehenge 'at its fullest development'. Impressions can be very powerful and leave strong, lasting images. Compare this image with others in the handbook. Was the circle ever complete? (see page 10).

success and technological crudity. The stones have also been the subject of much three-dimensional art – including some 'replicas' created in large scale out of cars and fridges! Children should be encouraged to research past artistic interpretations of the stones and – after sketching and/or photographing the stones on site – develop their own interpretations.

Music

The wind can make very peculiar sounds as it whistles through different landscapes. Wind instruments are based on the principle of controlling the rush of air across surfaces and through confined spaces. What music does the wind make in various parts of the open Stonehenge landscape? How does it contrast with wind music in the built environment? Children could experiment with different types of microphones to pick up wind music. What are the other common sounds in the Stonehenge landscape? During your visit get the children to note down the various sounds (and perhaps record some). Back at school they could create their own Stonehenge music (see the English Heritage video *Evidence of our lives* for a good example of music inspired by landscape).

Technology

The construction of Stonehenge, with its associated moving of hundreds of stones over very long distances, was an amazing piece of engineering. Children should research and discuss the types of technology used at Stonehenge (see pages 4 to 10). How does the technological development of a society influence other aspects of that society's development?

Maths and Science

Seen as a series of concentric circles Stonehenge sets a number of simple mathematical problems – for example, how do you lay out a circle on the ground and how do you space out regular intervals on that circle? Such work can also be extended into calculating the comparable forces and effort required to move stones (see pages 8 and 9).

The theory that Stonehenge is a complicated astronomical observatory is questioned and rejected by most archaeologists. However, there is little doubt that the monument is aligned on the axis of midsummer sunrise and midwinter sunset. Pupils could research some of the astronomical claims for Stonehenge (see Bibliography and resources) and discuss their probability. This could form the basis for an examination of the way our universe operates or the importance people attach(ed) to regularly observable cycles; cycles

Stonehenge by John Constable (1835). The painting was completed in the studio from a pencil sketch made fifteen years earlier.

that would have been especially critical for a society that relied entirely on the changing seasons without a full scientific understanding of the annual cycle.

Geography

It is generally accepted that the stones used in the construction of Stonehenge came from two sources a long way from where they were erected. Most archaeologists think that the bluestones were moved by water along the south coast of Wales, across the Bristol Channel and then by river and overland to Salisbury Plain and the sarsens transported overland all the way from the Marlborough Downs. However, it must be stressed that these are only ideas based on the shortest, probably easiest, routes.

Get your pupils to look closely at a map. What route would they chose to transport the bluestones to Stonehenge? They must be constrained by only using the

Experimental archaeology in practice: schoolboys working with Professor Stuart Atkinson move a stone by water in the 1950s.

23

A Druid celebration to mark a recent summer solstice. English Heritage allows special access, for anyone with a genuine interest, to the stone circle whenever possible.

material and equipment available to the original builders. They should remember that transport by sea is easier than on land, but there is a danger from storms and strong tides. When they have decided on the route get them to mark it on the map. How could they estimate how long the journey would take?

English

Children should be developing their language, recording and reporting (oral and written) skills throughout the project. Notes taken on their visit could form the basis of creative writing back at school, especially if your pupils are seeing the site for the first time, and time should be set aside for children to make notes on site. Role-play situations can be developed, for example, by giving a group the task of organizing the movement of bluestones from Wales. They should make a list of all the things they will need to complete the job successfully. What logistical problems will they have to overcome? Get them to describe their preparations and how all the people and animals involved in the operation are going to be organized, fed and rested on the journey. This work could be developed to create a whole prehistoric landscape with those organizing the construction of Stonehenge having to liaise with other groups/tribes – for example, the people who controlled the Preseli mountains and those who controlled the land between. Might the Stonehenge people have to accommodate a longer journey to avoid the territory of a group unsympathetic to the removal of the stones or the building of the monument?

Travel and Tourism

Group discussion before visiting the site can be used to produce a list of facilities that visitors to a site such as Stonehenge expect. What would the children themselves hope to see as visitor facilities at a World Heritage Site? Get them to develop lists of minimum requirements and compare this to their original lists (also see pages 28 and 32).

RE, Social Studies and Humanities

Over the years Stonehenge has mirrored social perceptions and provided a focus for our collective imagination; from religious monument and gathering place its purpose was lost and subsequently re-invented and mediated through Arthurian legend and untested antiquarian theories, progressively giving way to scientific archaeological interpretation over the last two centuries. Now, in the spiritual vacuum of the late twentieth century, it is once again claimed by some as a religious monument and gathering place. Before your visit get your pupils to discuss the varying pressures on the monument that result from it being different things to different people. (Also see pages 29 to 31.)

Providing refreshments for visitors is a full-time occupation.

Educational activities

Introduction

Some of the problems faced by the builders of Stonehenge can be discussed, and elaborated through simple experiments, in the classroom before your visit. These will help pupils to develop a fuller appreciation of the skills exercised by the builders of the monument and can also be used to introduce a wide range of cross-curricular work.

Throughout the activities you should stress to the children the need for them to accurately record all of their measurements and observations. Depending on their age, you could perhaps turn this into a role play exercise with the pupils taking on the role of archaeologists preparing a report on the possible construction techniques used at Stonehenge, or of the actual prehistoric builders trying to work out in

miniature how they are going to achieve the job they have been given. The children should work in groups with each group member taking it in turns to record the group's results. At the end of each stage the groups should have the opportunity to write up their results, perhaps using a word processor, or to present them to the whole class – and to be ready to defend their conclusions!

Building a brickhenge

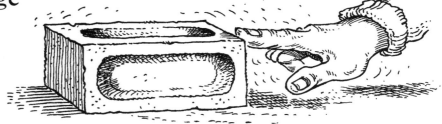

For this experiment you will need

- About 40 house bricks
- Parcel string
- Pencils or pieces of dowel to use as rollers
- Rubbers or small blocks of wood to use as fulcrums
- A variety of surfaces at least 1 metre long
- Spring balances
- A variety of small pulleys

It is not clear how, or by what route, the stones (each weighing between four and 50 tonnes) were actually transported to Stonehenge. The bluestones were probably moved as much as possible by water as this would have made their transportation easier. On land, both sets of stones

would have had to be pulled, probably on sledges or rollers (tree trunks), by teams of men or (now thought more likely) oxen, harnessed to the stones with ropes of leather or plant fibre. However they were moved, the operation was an enormous feat of engineering and organization. Even if animal power was used it has been estimated that the whole task of building just the final phase of Stonehenge took 1.5 million work hours.

Moving the stones

Each group should weigh one brick and measure its height, width and

length. The groups should then attempt to push the brick on a smooth, flat surface using only one child's finger tips to move it. They should record how many fingers were needed before the brick moved. Get them to try the same experiment on different surfaces recording how many fingers (effort) are needed for the different surfaces.

Give each group some string and suggest they try pulling the brick across the different surfaces and up – and down – various gradients. What happens when the slopes get steeper? The groups should use their spring balance to record how much pulling power they are using on each surface.

Get the groups to record what happens if they put wooden rollers (pencils) under their brick. Let them experiment by using different numbers of rollers. Does the number of rollers used make any difference to the amount of force needed to pull the brick? Do they have any problems using the rollers to move the bricks down the slope?

Get them to compare the weight of their bricks with some of the stones from Stonehenge. How many times heavier are the real

The 1950s excavation and consolidation work. Note the crane and also the wooden decking laid to protect the fragile below-ground archaeology.

stones? Can they calculate how much pulling power they think would have been needed to move the real stones?

Lifting the stones

Once at Stonehenge the stones had to be raised on end to form uprights or lifted high to act as lintels. Today we would use mechanically powered cranes to perform this work. The builders of Stonehenge had only earth, timber and ropes to do the job. How did they do it?

Get each group to devise a method for raising their bricks and then capping them with lintel bricks. They should be sure to use only that technology that was available to the builders of Stonehenge. How many different techniques have they used? Are any of them similar to the methods suggested on pages 8 and 9?

The body under the barrow

In September 1808 the antiquarian Sir Richard Colt Hoare excavated a barrow near Stonehenge called Bush Barrow. He made no drawings of what he found, but did leave a written description of his discoveries.

"... on reaching the floor of the barrow we discovered the skeleton ..., lying from south to north; the extreme length of his thigh bone was 20 inches. About 18 inches south of the head we found several brass rivets intermixed with wood...they were (probably) the moulded remains of a shield. Near the shoulders lay the fine celt (axe)...originally furnished with a handle of wood. Near the right arm was a large dagger of brass, and a spearhead of the same metal... These were accompanied by a curious article of gold which...had originally decorated the case of the dagger. The handle of wood belonging to this instrument exceeds anything we have yet seen...(the decoration) was formed...by thousands of gold rivets, smaller than the smallest pin. So very minute were these pins

Devizes Museum

Sir Richard Colt Hoare excavating a barrow near Stonehenge.

that our labourers had thrown out thousands of them with their shovels...before, by the necessary aid of magnifying glass, we could discover what they were, but fortunately enough remained attached to the wood to develop the pattern. Beneath the fingers of the right hand lay a lance of brass, but so much corroded that it broke to pieces on moving. Immediately over the breast of the skeleton was a large plate of gold in the form of a lozenge, measuring 7 inches by 6 inches. It was perforated at the top and bottom for the purpose of probably fastening it to the dress as a breast plate... We next discovered, on the right side of the skeleton, a very curious perforated stone, some articles of bone, many small rings of the same material, and another article of gold. The stone...had a wooden handle which was fixed into the perforation at the centre, and encircled by a neat ornament of brass, part of which still adheres to the stone."

Get your pupils to list all of the things they would like to know about someone who lived in the Bronze Age and who would have known all about Stonehenge and the beliefs that surrounded it. Then get them to read Colt Hoare's description carefully.

Initially get your pupils to answer factual questions about the burial. For example, what materials were used to make the objects buried with the body? Slowly develop the questions so they become more speculative, for example, what other materials that have not survived could have been with the body when it was buried? Develop the questions even further: Do they think the body is male or female? Why? How did he/she die? Was the person rich or poor? How do they know? Why do they think all

these things were buried with the body? Do they think all the objects were made by the dead person? Why?

Get the children to look at their original list. How many points can they answer using the evidence from the Bush Barrow excavation? How many more do they think they could answer had the body been excavated using modern scientific methods?

This activity could be developed by getting the children to think what things that they use every day would they have buried with them so that archaeologists in the future could dig them up and discover what their life was like? They could also use the evidence from Colt Hoare's description to make a drawing of the body and its grave goods to show what the burial might have looked like when it was first discovered.

Will the barrow survive?

Many of the burial mounds around Stonehenge have survived quite well in comparison with barrows elsewhere in England. Nevertheless, damage inflicted by rabbits and other burrowing animals, early excavations by antiquarians, long term ploughing, road widening, and the relatively new threat of extensive use of the area (whether for illegal festivals or mass tourism – see below) have all taken their toll. While your pupils are playing the game encourage them to discuss the reasons for their gaining or losing points.

The children will need a dice and a different coloured counter to represent each player's barrow.

START

Road widening destroys one side of the barrow. Lose 15 points.

1 **2** **3**

The land becomes sheep pasture protecting the barrow from further plough damage. Gain 5 points.

4 **5** **6** **7**

8

FINISH **38**

37 Early 18th century: Stukeley and the Earl of Pembroke open the barrow. All record of what they found is lost. Lose 10 points.

36

35

34

33

32

31 Landowner plants trees on the barrow. Their roots gradually burrow into the barrow damaging it. Lose 5 points.

30 English Heritage schedule the site protecting it from further damage. Gain 5 points.

29

28 Broken Beaker pottery found by Colt Hoare is thrown away by him as not being worth keeping. Lose 5 points.

27

26

25 **24** Early nineteenth century: Colt Hoare decides to investigate the barrow. His workmen dig down through the centre finding the central burial, but missing others in the mound and ditch. Lose 5 points.

23 **22** The barrow becomes a favourite picnic spot. People scrambling up and down the sides wear away the turf and increase erosion on the barrow. Lose 5 points.

21 Chemicals sprayed on the surrounding fields kill ancient flora growing on the barrow. Lose 5 points.

20 **19** **18**

9 Rabbits make a warren and damage the barrow with their digging. Lose 5 points.

10

11

Trees growing on top of the barrow are uprooted by a violent storm. This causes more damage to the barrow. Lose 5 points.

12

The National Trust buy the land on which the barrow sits and fence it off to reduce damage from **13** ploughing. Gain 5 points.

14

15

The farmer ploughs too close to the barrow and destroys the ditch and outer edges of the **16** mound. Lose 10 points.

An unthinking visitor breaks the law by using a metal detector on the barrow and digs in it in search of buried metal causing more damage. Lose 10 points.

17

Will the barrow survive?

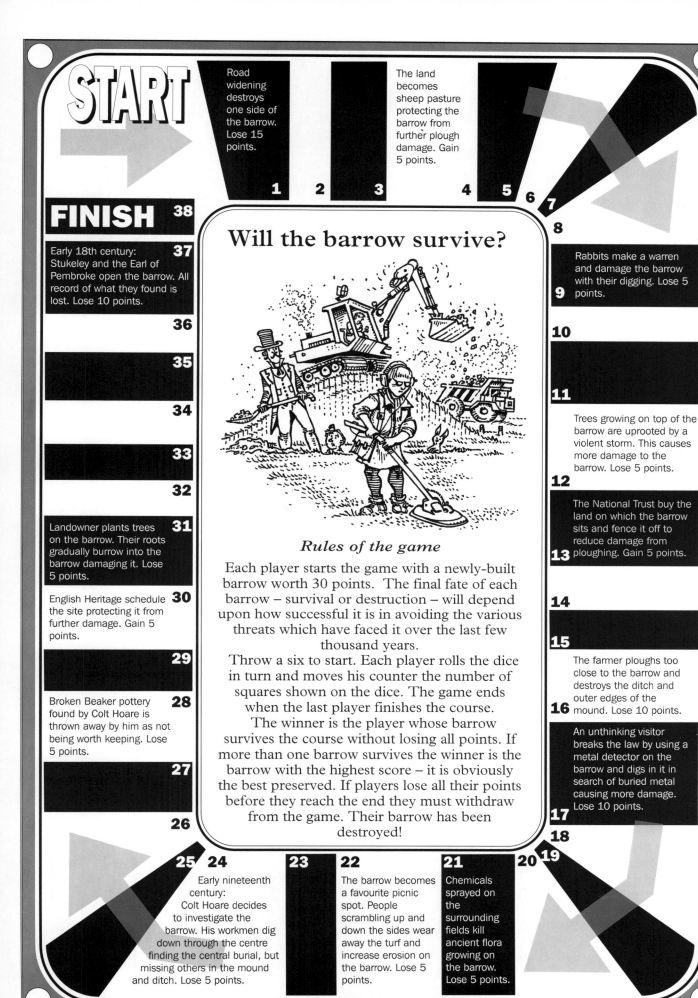

Rules of the game

Each player starts the game with a newly-built barrow worth 30 points. The final fate of each barrow – survival or destruction – will depend upon how successful it is in avoiding the various threats which have faced it over the last few thousand years.

Throw a six to start. Each player rolls the dice in turn and moves his counter the number of squares shown on the dice. The game ends when the last player finishes the course.

The winner is the player whose barrow survives the course without losing all points. If more than one barrow survives the winner is the barrow with the highest score – it is obviously the best preserved. If players lose all their points before they reach the end they must withdraw from the game. Their barrow has been destroyed!

Coping with visitors

Background

In the 1960s visitor numbers to Stonehenge rose to over 300,000 annually. To help provide a safer and more enjoyable visit the present underpass was built, the car park increased in size and toilets, souvenir and refreshment facilities improved. The present facilities are mainly housed within these 1960s improvements.

With the increasing number of visitors, the grass inside the stone circle became a muddy quagmire every time it rained and gravel was laid down to protect the remaining below-ground archaeology and to provide a less messy surface. However, the gravel stuck to people's shoes and began to damage the stones as they scrambled over them. Therefore, in 1978, the site was returned to grass and visitor access to the stones restricted.

Stonehenge today

In 1999-2000 some 836,000 visitors visited Stonehenge. Trapped as it is between two major trunk roads, probably almost as many viewed the stones from the dangers of the grass verge of the A344. The facilities for visitors and interpretation of the site are totally inadequate and are in desperate need of upgrading. Everyone concerned with the preservation, conservation and presentation of Stonehenge is convinced that the facilities and all the twentieth-century clutter should be moved outside the World Heritage Site in order for the stone circle to be returned to a grassland landscape, reunited with many of its associated prehistoric monuments and free from the noise, damage and intrusion of the two roads. The debate over the siting of any new visitor facilities, includes closing and grassing-over the A344, and the diversion of the A303 trunk road by either a long tunnel or a new road well to the north of Stonehenge.

The ground surface in the centre circle after a summer shower when visitors were allowed into the stones.

Visitor erosion

Before visiting Stonehenge get your pupils to look for evidence of wear and tear in and around the school. Which areas are worn/damaged – why? During the visit get them to collect evidence for effects of pressure of visitors on the site and the measures taken to prevent damage to the monument.

What do they think would happen to the Stonehenge circle if 800,000 visitors a year were all allowed to walk over it? What would they say to visitors who are disappointed not to be able to go into the monument and touch the stones? Or to the visitor who says that Stonehenge is very old and it should be allowed to wear out? Who, if anyone, do they think should be allowed into the stones?

Visitor facilities

Before the visit get your pupils to discuss the facilities they think

A recent experiment to find the hardest wearing grass for the path around the stones.

visitors to a World Heritage Site can expect to find. During their visit they should complete Activity Sheet 2. Back in the classroom pupils should write up and discuss their results. Are the facilities adequate for the needs of the visitor? Were all the facilities they originally listed available? What was missing? Why was it missing? – what are the constraints of the site? Could any further improvements be made on the present site? If a new visitor centre could be built and equipped regardless of cost what would they put into it? Note that all the unique finds from the area are presently dispersed – mainly in Salisbury and Devizes museums. Do different visitors have different needs: for example, school groups, foreign tourists, disabled visitors? How realistic do they think their ideas are? What are the criteria for how much money could be spent on such a new centre?

Who owns Stonehenge?

The simple answer to this is "we do": Stonehenge, and the small triangle of land in which it stands, was given to the nation in 1918 by the then owner Cecil Chubb. This ownership is held on behalf of the nation by the Secretary of State for National Heritage and is managed on a daily basis by English Heritage. Most of the land around this small area now belongs to the National Trust.

Most modern visitors simply want to come to Stonehenge to see what many regard as one of the wonders of the world. Many are disappointed that they cannot wander peacefully amongst the stones, taking their own photos and quietly pondering why they were erected and by what type of people: but nearly all accept the conservation and preservation problems that keep them on the pathway twenty or so metres away from the stones.

For anyone who, for whatever reason, desperately wants to actually go inside the stone circle such restriction is enormously frustrating. English Heritage attempts to satisfy as many people as possible who really want to go into the stone circle by granting special 'out-of-hours' access when the monument is usually closed. Over the last few years archaeologists, ley liners, Druids, educational parties, advertising agencies, New Age travellers, military units stationed near-by, local people and small family groups who just want to get into the centre circle, are amongst those who have been granted such special access. Effectively the only restrictions are that groups are usually limited to no more than twenty five, that they enter the circle before or after normal opening times and, of course, that they do no damage to the monument. A few people are not content with these arrangements. What follows is a simplified set of arguments about this 'ownership' debate. It is included here in order to stimulate children to begin to think about and discuss this type of

The stones have long been a magnet for graffiti and anyone wanting to bring their cause to the eyes of the nation. Such graffiti causes long term damage to old and rare lichens.

'heritage issue'. Such issues are never clear-cut. However, if we do not address them we run the risk of them getting out of hand and perhaps becoming even more problematic.

Background

Although it is clear that Stonehenge was abandoned centuries before anything like a Druid appeared anywhere near what we now call Salisbury Plain, by the early twentieth century modern Druids were holding regular ceremonies at Stonehenge to coincide with the midsummer solstice.

As time passed increasingly large crowds gathered to watch these modern Druids perform their ceremonies. As dawn drew near people scrambled up onto the stones for a better view and there were fears for the continued stability of the stones and safety of the spectators. The increasingly large crowds also brought problems of policing and crowd control and created a considerable litter problem: in 1961 broken bottles alone filled eight wheel barrows.

By the late 1970s these solstice gatherings had increased dramatically in size and the pirate station Radio Caroline had begun to advertise the "Stonehenge People's Free Festival." Although people camped illegally on National Trust land the Trust allowed the festival to continue. In 1984 there were an estimated 30,000+ participants, many camping illegally on National Trust land for up to six weeks. By this time the festival also featured a stage and live rock bands.

In the early summer of 1985, following damage during the previous year's festival, and because of increasing fears for the safety of the large crowds, the National Trust, supported by English Heritage, decided that no further festivals would be held on its land. Other local landowners were equally unwilling to play host to the festival goers. As the stone circle was seen as the focus for the festival no special out-of-hours access was allowed to the site for the summer solstice and, after consultation with the police, the unprecedented decision was taken to close the monument for two days over the solstice.

This decision was challenged by the Festival organisers on the grounds that it flaunted the conditions of Cecil Chubb's original gift of the site to the nation. It was also argued that Stonehenge was now simply a money-making attraction for tourists who should not be put off visiting at the height of the season by the sight of dishevelled campers in the surrounding fields. When it became clear that the organisers intended to go ahead with the festival court injunctions were taken out against the 84 people who were considered active in promoting the event. Wiltshire police spent £1 million in fighting and winning the so-called 'Battle of Stonehenge' and preventing the festival from taking place.

A similar, but smaller scale confrontation took place in 1986. In 1988 English Heritage offered 1000 free tickets to anyone who wanted to be at Stonehenge for the Summer Solstice but only about half of these were taken up. However, an estimated 5000 people walked to the stones on the night of the solstice and attempted to force their way in to the site. Over 1000 police were called in from 17 different forces and the Chief Constable of Wiltshire actually read the Riot Act to the crowd from the safety of a helicopter hovering overhead.

Until 1998 there was no special out-of-hours access granted at the summer solstice. Subsequent solstices passed more peacefully but the problem of access remained. The situation was unsatisfactory for all interested groups. From the mid 1990s English Heritage started a dialogue with many of these different special interest groups, like the travelling community, pagans and Druid orders. Some had formerly been protagonists and it took time to develop a mutually trusting relationship. This resulted in Managed Open Access being possible at the Summer Solstice in 2000. This meant anybody could have free open access.

The enormous volume of newspaper articles on conflict at Stonehenge makes this an ideal subject for studying conflict in society and media presentation itself. The presence of the monument amidst one of the highest concentrations of military installations in England makes the Stonehenge landscape a very sensitive security area. At the same time young people seek security of a different sort in Stonehenge (see Sid Rawle's letter in the documentary sources).

Get your pupils to act out a debate with a number of the interested parties present. Different groups of children could be tasked to research the background arguments for different parties – some notes follow to help with this. A further group could act as a jury. Which arguments are strongest? What do the children conclude should happen?

National Trust
The Trust owns most of the land around Stonehenge. It was bought to safeguard the archaeological monuments that can be seen above the ground and to protect the archaeology beneath the ground. We try to allow as much access as possible to our land and this is why we did not immediately stop the Stonehenge festival in the 1970s. However, things got out of hand: too many people wanted to camp in too small an area for too long a time with too few facilities. As owners we are ultimately responsible for people on our land – whether we invite them on or not. The festival had to be stopped as we could not guarantee the safety of those attending the festival or of the above or below ground archaeology. We would be keen for English Heritage to allow special access to the stones again at the solstice, and are keen to support them in their efforts (see below).

English Heritage
We supported the National Trust in their decision to stop the illegal festival on their land – which is part of a World Heritage Site, designated as such by UNESCO because of its unique archaeological importance. After consultation with the police we have also stopped special out-of-hours access to Stonehenge at the summer solstice. Stonehenge is really very small. Too many people want to come at the same time for us to be able to offer adequate crowd protection or adequate protection to the monument. The last time people invaded the stones at one of these events, one of the stones was quite badly gouged. We are also concerned that any unusual action, such as people climbing on them, may destabilise the stones. We would like to allow special access at these events again but everybody has to agree how this can be achieved. As yet, we do not have a consensus – the Druids cannot even agree amongst themselves – but we will continue to work towards it.

District Council
The District Council is the authority which, at the request of the police, considers whether to make Orders prohibiting groups of 20 or more people gathering together and trespassing on the Stonehenge site at times such as the summer solstice. Such gatherings have happened in the past and caused disruption to the local community and expense, in police costs, to local tax payers.

Local landowner
I farm land close to Stonehenge and really do not want a free festival anywhere near my land. It brings in too many people who do not understand that those fields are my livelihood: if they trample the crops (and don't forget the festival always used to be in June) they can cause thousands of pounds worth of damage. Not to mention them collecting wood from everywhere for their camp fires – from my woods and by knocking down my fences. And the mess they leave behind. No. I'm not against festivals: but not here. Anyway, what about all the damage they do to the archaeology?

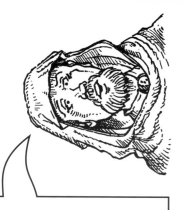

Druid
It has never been proved that Druids ever worshipped at Stonehenge. Nor is the summer solstice a particularly important time for Druids. Druids are the "Oak people" and it was in private in clearings under oak trees that the earliest Druids taught their followers. We are only referred to as "pagan" because that is how the Romans described us. We are a non-religious, non-political body and have many Christians amongst our members. The most important time of the year is in early December when mistletoe, our most important medicine, is around. What happens at Stonehenge in June at the moment is madness and is just nothing to do with real Druid beliefs.

Druid 2
We are the descendants of those people who built Stonehenge and other similar monuments. We still follow the ancient, pagan religion of Druidism and feel aggrieved and wronged that we cannot go into our most important temple at the most important time of the year for us. We believe Stonehenge to be our pagan temple; why should we be locked out of our most important place of worship? It is like Christians being locked out of St Paul's Cathedral at Christmas. We do not necessarily agree with many of those who want to hold the festival, as the problems surrounding it have caused us to be excluded from Stonehenge when we want to be there the most.

Police
The role of the police is to uphold the law and to maintain public order. In 1985 the National Trust decided not to allow what was in effect an illegal festival to take place on their land as had happened over the previous few years. These festivals have led to many public order problems that resulted in the ban. We understand that the National Trust and English Heritage have responsibilities to make such difficult but necessary decisions. We also understand the views of the majority of local farmers and many local residents who do not want the festival to take place.

New Age Traveller
I just want to be left alone to do what I want to do and go where I want to go. I think Stonehenge is special and I want to be allowed to go there at the solstice and have a good time – after all, it was probably a festival site when it was built. We believe they have just made it into a tourist attraction so they can make money out of it: they've ripped the soul out of the site and made it just a commercial venture – just like Disneyland. Anyway, who are these archaeologists who claim to know what went on there? They don't agree anyway. How do they know the Druids didn't build it; they weren't there? Stonehenge belongs to the nation: that's you and me.

New visitor facilities

In 1993, before the possible changes to the A303 really came into the equation, English Heritage and the National Trust looked at a number of possible sites for new visitor facilities. The following activity looks at five of these possible sites and requires pupils to assess their viability against a set of specified criteria. All of the sites assume that the A344 will be closed – a move against the wishes of some local people who complain that they will have to travel further to give tourists a better experience. It can be assumed for the activity that the same new visitor facilities would be built at each location – thus removing any difference in cost, other than road building and any necessary ongoing transportation costs.

Get your pupils to balance the above factors for each site and suggest which is the most suitable location.

Assessment Criteria

1 Quality of the approach to the stones, and through this the quality of the whole experience.

2 New access roads required for the facilities must be kept to the absolute minimum especially if their route crosses into the World Heritage Site. They should not, if at all possible, damage any archaeology.

3 Archaeological sensitivity. Today archaeologists prefer not to excavate unless they have to and so the more archaeology that remains undisturbed the better.

4 Distance from the stones. What is the maximum distance people can be reasonably expected to walk? Is it fair to keep lazy people or people on tight schedules away from the stones? Provision for the elderly and disabled must be made, which will probably mean an artificial surface and some form of transport, possibly powered electrically.

The five possible locations

Countess Road East The only practical site outside the World Heritage Site and the only site which would allow a full range of the latest presentational, educational, retail and restaurant facilities for the visitor. It is separated from the historic landscape by the A345. A building here would have to tackle the noise of the A303 and incorporate the service buildings at Countess roundabout. Road access is straightforward. Its distance from Stonehenge means that 'park-and-ride' is the only viable way to visit the monument.

Fargo South A building here would involve a southerly extension to the Fargo Plantation to screen the visitor centre and car parking. Access is from the tail of the A344. The distance of the walk to Stonehenge is reasonable but the land is archaeologically very sensitive. From the site there is an unprepossessing view of the stones with a wood behind them and an aircraft hanger on the horizon above. An approach to the stones via a shallow valley does improve this.

Larkhill The new approach road (which uses the line of an existing road for part of its length) could, in itself, be a scenic experience through the landscape. This is one of the least archaeologically sensitive sites within the World Heritage Site. The approach to the stones is spectacular but the site is small and there would be difficulties in providing a full range of interpretational facilities.

New King Barrows Close to Amesbury and a fine eastern entrance to the landscape with a wonderful 360 degree view over it. There would be great difficulty with this site depending on which of a number of possible new routes for the A303 is chosen. The most sensitive site archaeologically – which would seriously constrain the development of the site.

Old King Barrows Less sensitive archaeologically, this site gives an excellent approach to Stonehenge on or beside 'The Avenue', but the approach is rather long and a rebuilt road would be needed from the Countess roundabout, along the existing Countess track.

The Visitor Centre: Comparison of Alternative Sites (1993)

Site Barrows	Countess Road East	Fargo South	Larkhill	New King Barrows	Old King
Sensitivity of archaeology	🏛	🏛🏛🏛	🏛🏛	🏛🏛🏛	🏛🏛
Length of access road from public highway (km)	0.1	1.2	2.9	0.1	1.7
Length of walk to the stones (km)	3.6	1.1	1.0	1.0	1.3
Order of costs £m	14.5	13.75	16.5	14.5	14.5
Quality of approach	☆	☆	☆☆☆	☆☆☆	☆☆

Activity Sheet 1: **The stones of Stonehenge**

Look at the pieces of bluestone and sarsen which have been set up near the entrance to the monument. Record similarities and differences in colour and texture between the two types of rock on the table below. What other characteristics can you add to the table to identify differences between the stones?

	Bluestone	Sarsen
Colour		
Texture		

? Is it possible, other than by their size, to tell bluestones apart from sarsen stones?

. . . .

? Have you seen any stone suitable for building in the area of Stonehenge?

. . . .

? Why do you think people built a stone monument where there was no stone?

. . . .

Take photographs and make sketches of the stone circle to remind yourself of what the monument looks like.

Activity Sheet 2: **Visitor facilities**

You have been hired by English Heritage to write a report on the present visitor facilities. Study the facilities that are on site and complete (and extend) the table below.

facility	not adequate	adequate	good	very good	excellent
signage to the site					
shop					

Take photographs or make sketches to illustrate your report.

Heritage Consultants Ltd
Report to English Heritage on visitor facilities at Stonehenge

Bibliography and resources

Stonehenge

Probably more has been written about Stonehenge than any other site in Britain. As long ago as 1900 a bibliography for the site contained almost 1000 references. What follows is by no means an exhaustive list, but a recommended series of starting points. Teachers requiring more detailed references are referred to Chippindale 1994.

Atkinson, R.J.C. *Stonehenge: archaeology and interpretation*, Penguin, 1979, ISBN 0-14-020450-4.
Atkinson, R.J.C. *Stonehenge and neighbouring monuments*, English Heritage, 1995, 1-85074-172-7.
Barrett, J.C., *Fragments from Antiquity*, Oxford, Blackwells, 1994, ISBN 0-631-18954-8.
Chippindale, C. et al. *Who Owns Stonehenge?* Batsford, 1990, ISBN 0-7134-6455-0.
Chippindale, C. *Stonehenge complete*, Thames and Hudson, 1994, ISBN 0-500-277350-8.
Grinsell, L.V. *Legendary history and folklore of Stonehenge*, 1975. (Sold in bookshop at Salisbury and South Wiltshire Museum.)
Richards, J. *Beyond Stonehenge: a guide to Stonehenge and its prehistoric landscape*, Trust for Wessex Archaeology, 1985, ISBN 0-9509981-2-5. (Available from Stonehenge shop.)
Richards, J. *Stonehenge*, Batsford, 1991, ISBN 0-7134-6142-X.

Books for teachers

Burl, A. *Prehistoric stone circles*, Shire, 1979, ISBN 0-85263-457-7.
Burl, A. *Prehistoric astronomy and ritual*, Shire, 1983, ISBN 0-85263-621-0.
Coupland, L. *The Avebury monuments: a study pack for teachers*, English Heritage, 1988, ISBN 1-85074-173-5.
Darvill, T. *Prehistoric Britain*, Batsford, 1987, ISBN 0-7134-5179-3.
Renfrew, J. *Food and cooking in prehistoric Britain*, English Heritage, 1985, ISBN 1-85074-533-1.

Educational Approaches

Copeland, T, *A Teacher's Guide to Geography and the Historic Environment*, English Heritage, 1993, ISBN 1-85074-332-0.
Copeland, T, *A Teacher's Guide to Maths and the Historic Environment*, English Heritage, 1992, ISBN 1-85074-329-0.
Corbishley, M, Darvill, T and Stone, P, *Prehistory, A Teachers Guide*, English Heritage, 2000, ISBN 1-85074-325-8.
Fairclough, J and Redsell, P, *A Teacher's Guide to History through Role Play*, English Heritage, 1994, ISBN 1-85074-478-5.
Keen, J, *A Teachers Guide to Ancient Technology*, English Heritage, 1996, ISBN 1-85074-448-3.
Maddern, E, *A Teacher's Guide to Storytelling at Historic Sites*, English Heritage, 1992, ISBN 1-85074-378-9.

Two gentlemen stroll among the stones in the nineteenth century.

English Heritage

The shop at Stonehenge sells a wide range of quality books, souvenirs and gifts to suit every pocket.

children can develop skills by recording, researching and interpreting their local environment.

A wide range of English Heritage videos are available: please see the **Resources** catalogue for details.

Museums

Wiltshire Heritage Museum has a display of archaeological material from sites in Wiltshire. Pre-booking for education groups is essential and an admission charge is payable. Tel. 01380-727369.
Salisbury and South Wiltshire Museum has a display of the archaeological material from Stonehenge and its environs, including Durrington Walls. There is also a display of paintings and other 2-dimensional images of Stonehenge. Pre-booking for education groups is essential and an admission charge is payable. Tel. 01722-332151.

Acknowledgements

Thanks go to Janet Bell, Clare Conybeare and Julian Richards.

Pownall, J, and Hutson, N, *A Teacher's Guide to Science and the Historic Environment*, English Heritage, 1992, ISBN 1-85074-331-2.

Books for pupils

Reference

Branigan, K. *Prehistory*, Kingfisher Books, 1984, ISBN 0-86272-090-7.

Corbishley, M. *Prehistoric Britain Activity Book*, British Museum Publications, 1989, ISBN 0-7141-1394-8.

Corbishley, M. *What do we know about prehistoric people?*, Simon Schuster, 1994, ISBN 0-7500-1324-9.

Crystal, D. and Foster, J. *The Stone Age*, Arnold, 1985, ISBN 0-7131-7300-9.

Dawson, I. *Prehistoric Britain*, Holmes McDougal, 1983, ISBN 0-7157-2133-X.

Grant, J. *The Neolithic revolution*, Holmes McDougal, 1984, ISBN 0-7157-2136-4.

Herdman, M. *Hunters and early farmers in Britain*, Nelson, 1985, ISBN 0-174-44213-0.

Fiction

Burnham, J and Ray, T. *Children of the stones*, Carousel, 1977, ISBN 0-552-52067-5.

Christopher, J. *Dom and Va*,
Hamish Hamilton, 1979, ISBN 0-241-02329-7.

Fidler, K. *The boy with the bronze axe*, Puffin, 1968, ISBN 0-14-030563-7.

Sutcliff, R. *Warrior scarlet*, Puffin, 1958, ISBN 014-030895-4.

Treece, H. *The Dream Time*, Heinemann, 1974, ISBN 0-435-12196-0.

Walsh, J.P. *The Dawnstone*, Piccolo, 1973, ISBN 0-330-25735-8.

Woodbridge, T. *Sheldra. A child in Neolithic Orkney*, Tempus Reparatum, 1988, ISBN 1-871314-003.

Videos

Archaeology at Work, English Heritage, 1994. Key stages 2 and 3; In-service teacher training; adult education, 58 minutes.

This is a new series of videos that introduce the equipment and methods used by archaeologists today from excavation and fieldwork to scientific techniques; from conservation in the laboratory to the management of our historic environment.
Evidence of our lives, English Heritage, 1991. Key stages 2 and 3, 27 minutes.

This video, divided into short sections, looks at the nature of physical evidence. It shows how

English Heritage Education
We aim to help teachers at all levels to use the resource of the historic environment. Each year, we welcome half a million pupils, students and teacher on free educational group visits to over 400 historic sites in our care. We also offer services to help access the National Monuments Record, our public archive. For free copies of our **Free Educational Visits** booklet, our **Resources** catalogue, and **Heritage Learning**, our termly magazine, contact:

**English Heritage Education
Freepost 22 (WD214)
London W1E 7EZ
Tel: 0870 333 1181**

E-mail: education@english-heritage.org.uk

www.english-heritage.org.uk/education

Back cover: Stonehenge in the snow. (English Heritage)